INDOOR GARDENING FOR BROWN THUMBS

HERBS

by Gary M. Spahl

Illustrated by
Kathleen Estes

BRISTOL PUBLISHING ENTERPRISES
San Leandro, California

Printed in Singapore.

ISBN 1-55867-185-4

CONTENTS

YOU <u>CAN</u> GROW HERBS INDOORS!   1

HERBS: THE KITCHEN TREASURES   5

     Basil 9

     Sage 13

     Rosemary 16

     Chives 20

     Dill 23

     Oregano 26

     Thyme 29

     Tarragon 32

     Mint 35

     Marjoram 39

     Parsley 42

     Cilantro 46

HOW TO CHOOSE AN HERB PLANT   49

MORE ABOUT CARE OF HERBS .   53

HARVESTING AND STORING HERBS   79

CONTAINERS; DECORATING TIPS   83

BIBLIOGRAPHY 86

INDEX 87

Look for other books
in this series.

Indoor Gardening For Brown Thumbs

**HANGING PLANTS
TOUGHEST HOUSEPLANTS
FLOWERING HOUSEPLANTS
HERBS
LARGE FLOOR PLANTS
PLANTS FOR DARK CORNERS**

for a free catalog, call or write

Bristol Publishing Enterprises
800 346-4889
in California
510 895-4461
P.O. Box 1737
San Leandro, CA 94577

YOU <u>CAN</u> GROW HERBS INDOORS!

You can cook up a storm. You can tell the difference between Parsley, Sage, Rosemary and Thyme — and you know how and when to use them. Like all good cooks, you know that "fresh is best," so you want to grow your own herbs. But even though you can roast a leg of lamb that would make a Greek tycoon weep, you can't grow a plant to save your life. You've been peeling those potatoes with a brown thumb.

Don't be discouraged; there is hope. You don't have to limit yourself to anemic dried Chives or a five-dollar sprig of packaged fresh Rosemary. This book has instructions on how to grow twelve different herbs that I call the *Kitchen Treasures*. Just follow the tips on light, watering and fertilizer, and you'll soon be tossing fresh, aromatic leaves into your food with carefree abandon. I've also included hints on harvesting and storing your herbs, which is important since you'll be growing bumper crops.

I've been accused more than once of being a bit cynical, but I do admit to having a romantic fondness for fresh herbs. They have a mystical quality that has evolved over much time and use. Centuries ago some herbs were thought to have magical powers. They've been used for baths, perfumes, potpourris and in cooking to soothe or invigorate both spirits and emotions.

Cast a Spell on Your Soup Pot

Herbal power may not just be the stuff of Merlin and old wives' tales. While the psychology of scent is still largely uncharted, tests have shown that it can affect mood and emotion. People still study herbs and use them for healing body and mind — and even a little magic. A friend of mine burned Sage to clear her home of evil spirits. (I'm not sold on this one. She ended up moving out.)

The Kitchen Treasures in this book are primarily for cooking. Like other herbs, their flavors and aromas have a powerful effect on the brain. Herbs growing on a windowsill bring delicious aromas into your home. Putting fresh herbs into food engages both smell and taste to provide a deeper experience. So if you find yourself sighing with contentment while eating a fresh Basil alfredo sauce, you may be experiencing what's been known about this herb since the days of Nero.

Okay, enough romanticism. Whether you want to perk up your cooking or scare away a few spirits, there are plenty of herbs here for you to choose from. So clean off a nice, sunny windowsill; you're going to be growing some pots of lush, beautiful, fragrant herbs. Your life may never be the same again.

HERBS:
THE KITCHEN TREASURES

Right now, you have little jars filled with dried leaves on your kitchen shelf. Maybe you've purchased a few fresh herbs, lying in their little refrigerated plastic beds. Now it's time to grow your own Kitchen Treasures: living herbs will add zest to your food and your home, and dollars to your pocket.

The twelve herbs described in this book represent a symphony of flavors and aromas, from the cooling taste of Mint to the heady scent of Sage. The plants also provide a variety of foliage, from feathery, light green Dill and silvery-blue Tarragon to bushy, robust Basil. While these plants are individuals, they're all pretty easy to care for. Make sure they get plenty of light and water, and you'll be ready to turn your everyday meal into a culinary masterpiece.

Each plant has an illustration and brief description to help you recognize it, since you may not be used to seeing it alive and kicking. Basic care symbols illustrate how much effort a plant requires, while other symbols show how much water and light it needs. There are also symbols that indicate if the plant will last one season or keep producing for several years.

BASIC CARE SYMBOLS

 <u>Very Easy Care</u>. If you want to water a plant once a week, look for this symbol.

 <u>Easy Care</u>. If you can water a little more frequently, go for a plant with this symbol.

 <u>Light Active Care</u>. If you can not only water, but occasionally prune or divide, give this symbol a try.

WATER SYMBOLS

 <u>Moderate</u>. The top inch of soil will be dry for a day or two. Weekly watering should be fine.

 <u>Wet</u>. The soil should be kept consistently moist. Water at least weekly and check every few days. Give a light watering if the soil surface feels dry.

LIGHT SYMBOLS

 <u>Moderate light</u>. This would be some distance away from east, west or south windows, or closer if curtains filter the light. You could cast a dim shadow on plants in moderate light.

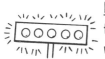 <u>Bright light</u>. These conditions are found close to east, west and south windows, and there may be times when the area gets direct sunlight. Most herbs prefer at least several hours a day of full sun.

PLANT DURATION SYMBOLS

 <u>Annual</u>. Like garden plants that are killed by the first frost, these herbs will lose their vigor within a year. Discard and start again with a new young plant.

 <u>Perennial</u>. With proper care, these herbs will keep growing for years.

Use the symbols to help you decide which plants to buy. But keep in mind that the most important factor in growing herbs is not how much care they need, but whether you like the smell and taste of the herb. You may appreciate Oregano's wild, sprawling nature and have the right temperament to care for it, but if you won't use it, what's the point?

Each herb plant also has notes on feeding, pruning and harvesting. Additional tips on these and other topics begin on page 53, **More About Care of Herbs**. But now, let's discover the Kitchen Treasures!

BASIL

Easy Care

Wet

Bright, Full Sun

Annual

Basil is a very popular herb. The bushy character and lush leaves make an attractive plant. Different varieties have different flavors. Best when used fresh.

This tasty herb has a long and checkered history. People in the Middle Ages thought scorpions bred underneath pots of Basil, and the early Greeks believed that the strong scent could drive a person insane. Looking at insanity in a different light, Basil was a symbol of love in Italy. A man would wear a sprig in his hair to announce his romantic intentions. Today, aromatherapists use Basil to cheer the heart and mind. Whether you believe in the psychology of scent or not, I know that a salad of garden tomatoes, basil and good olive oil always puts me in a good space.

There are several varieties of Basil, each with a different appearance and taste. *Sweet* or *Italian Basil* is probably the most familiar. The smooth green leaves are shaped like a fat, pointed oval. *Lemon Basil* has tiny, pointed leaves with a tart, citrus-like flavor. *Thai Basil* has narrow, dark green leaves; the taste is very earthy and almost hot. All types of Basil will send up stalks tipped with small white or purple flowers and will grow between 15 and 24 inches tall.

Basil is available as small plants and can also be grown from seed. Follow the instructions on the seed packet, and check page 67 for other tips. This plant is an annual and will lose its vigor after several months.

Plant Basil seeds throughout the year for a continuous crop.

Light Requirements for Basil

Basil needs four to six hours of full sun a day for best growth.

Watering Basil

Water every five to seven days, and pour off any water remaining in the drainage saucer after 20 minutes. Check the soil regularly with your finger to make sure it's moist. Don't let the soil dry out, or the leaves can become bitter.

Feeding Basil

Feed plants every two to three weeks, and never use more fertilizer than recommended on the package. For more about plant food, see page 59.

Pinching and Pruning Basil

Pinch off the tops of branches when the plant is about four inches tall; then pinch periodically to sustain bushy growth. Pinch off flower stalks to keep new leaves sprouting.

Harvesting and Storing Basil

Basil is best used fresh. It can be harvested when plants are at least four inches tall. Pick individual leaves, and use branch tips that are pinched off as well. The leaves darken quickly after being cut. Basil tends to lose its flavor when dried, but it does freeze well. See page 79 for more tips.

SAGE

 Very Easy Care

 Moderate

 Bright, Full Sun

 Perennial

Sage is a very flavorful herb that's also a beautiful plant. Leaf color can be gray-green, purple, gold, red or cream. Needs lots of sun. Can be used fresh or dried.

Everyone in America must have smelled this herb at least once a year. When you take a hearty whiff of the stuffing from the Thanksgiving turkey, that tantalizing aroma is Sage. In the American Southwest and the Mediterranean, you can smell Sage growing on the hillsides. The scent is rich and satisfying, but I've finished more than one hike with a mad craving for a turkey dinner with all the trimmings. For centuries Sage has been considered a remedy for poor digestion. Without Sage in the stuffing, you'd probably feel even more full and sleepy after that Thanksgiving feast!

Sage is a beautiful, shrub-like plant that can reach two feet tall. The leaves are oblong, two to four inches long and a bit woolly, growing on hairy stems. The most colorful of the Kitchen Treasures, the leaves are usually a soft gray-green, but different varieties are red, purple, gold, cream or a combination. Spikes of purplish, pink or white flowers will appear in late spring or early summer.

Sage takes two years to mature from seed, so grow it from small starter plants. This herb is a perennial and can be divided in the spring to create more plants and maintain hardy growth. See page 74 for tips on dividing plants.

Light Requirements for Sage

For best growth, Sage needs six to eight hours of sun each day.

Watering Sage

Water weekly, and pour off any water left in the drainage saucer after 20 minutes.

Feeding Sage

Fertilize plants once in the spring when new growth appears. Never use more fertilizer than the manufacturer recommends. See page 59 for more about plant food.

Pinching and Pruning Sage

Each spring, cut back the previous year's growth by half. This will stimulate vigorous new growth.

Harvesting and Storing Sage

Harvest when the plant has at least two inches of new growth. Pick leaves anytime to use fresh. To dry, cut six- to eight-inch sections off stems just as the flower buds appear. For more on drying herbs, go to page 81.

ROSEMARY

 Very Easy Care

 Moderate

 Moderate to Bright, Full Sun

 Perennial

Rosemary is a very pretty plant with a solid yet delicate profile. Very fragrant but a bit sticky. Can be used fresh or dried.

This is the most romantic of the Kitchen Treasures. The name is so pretty, and probably everyone has met a Rosemary who was a sweet, wonderful person. The Latin name *Rosemarinus* means *sea dew*, likely resulting from the Mediterranean hills where the plant grows wild and is often dusted with mist from the sea. Because the strong scent is believed to awaken the mind, Rosemary is considered the herb of remembrance. In Europe some brides carry a sprig in their bouquets. In America, you can tie a sprig on your husband's side of the bed a few days before your anniversary.

Rosemary has many thin, straight, woody stems that make a very dense shrub. The needle-like leaves grow from less than an inch to two inches. Dark, emerald green on top and white on the underside, the leaves feel slightly oily. Your fingers will carry the piney scent after touching the leaves. Tiny, pale blue flowers appear at different times of the year, depending on the climate. The plants may not bloom indoors.

Grown indoors, Rosemary will get between two and three feet tall. A variety known as *Prostrate Rosemary* is a trailing plant with softer, rambling stems, but just as much flavor and aroma.

It takes about two years for a Rosemary plant to mature from seed, so buy small plants instead. This plant does best with the roots a bit crowded. Repot every two years and divide the plant to keep it growing strong. See page 74 for tips.

Light Requirements for Rosemary
Rosemary does best with at least four hours of sun a day, but can tolerate moderate light.

Watering Rosemary
Water every seven to ten days. Pour off any drainage water left in the saucer after 20 minutes. Let the soil become fairly dry between waterings.

Feeding Rosemary
Fertilize Rosemary every two to three weeks. Never use more fertilizer than the package recommends. See page 59 for more tips.

Pinching and Pruning Rosemary
Rosemary grows slowly indoors. Harvesting stem tips should accomplish any pruning needs. If your plant is growing too tall, just cut the stems back with sharp scissors.

Harvesting and Storing Rosemary

For fresh Rosemary, leaves can be removed at any time after the plant has shown two inches of new growth. To harvest for drying, cut stems just before the flowers bloom. See page 79 for more tips on harvesting and storing herbs.

CHIVES

Very Easy Care

Moderate

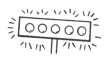
Bright, Full Sun

Perennial

The Chives plant is delicate-looking with pretty, edible flowers. Easy to harvest and very prolific. Best when used fresh.

What's a baked potato without sour cream and Chives? What are potato skins without sour cream and Chives? Heck, what's sour cream without Chives? Those tiny little tubes have a sweet, oniony flavor that can add a little pep to salads, dressings, eggs or soft cheese spreads. And they're a quick way to make almost anything look more elegant. Sprinkle a few fresh chives on a packaged frozen Salisbury steak dinner and the kids will think it's a company dinner.

A Chives plant has dainty, thin, straw-like leaves bursting up from the soil in dense clumps. This plant is a member of the onion family and grows eight to twelve inches tall from small bulbs. In springtime, small bulb-like flower buds spring up on thin stems, and then burst into small purple or pink powder-puffs. The flowers are attractive enough to cut for arrangements, and make a pretty garnish for food.

Chives are slow to mature from seed; it's best to buy a small starter plant. Every two years divide the plant to keep it growing strong and to create more plants. Turn to page 75 for tips on dividing chives.

Light Requirements for Chives
Chives do best with at least four hours of sunlight each day.

Watering Chives

Water once a week, and pour off any water remaining in the drainage saucer after 20 minutes.

Feeding Chives

Fertilize Chives once or twice a year if the plant seems to be a little sluggish. Never use more fertilizer than recommended by the manufacturer. For more tips, turn to page 59.

Pinching and Pruning Chives

Chives don't branch, so pinching and pruning aren't necessary.

Harvesting and Storing Chives

Chives are best used fresh; they don't dry well. Just snip the leaves off with scissors as you need them. The flowers are also flavorful.

DILL

 Very Easy Care

 Moderate

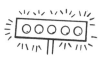 Bright, Full Sun

 Annual

Dill doesn't need much care, but indoor plants don't fare as well as garden-grown plants. Leaves are best used fresh. Dried seeds provide a different dimension of flavor.

Dill has been used for centuries, and is respected for its effectiveness in cooking, medicine and matters of the spirit. It grows wild in many areas of the world, and was cultivated in ancient Greece and Babylonia. In the Middle Ages, sprigs of Dill were worn and hung in houses to protect against evil spells. Next time you have to entertain difficult family members or business associates, whip up some cream cheese and fresh dill spread — and wear a sprig to keep yourself safe.

The feathery leaves of Dill make this a very elegant and attractive plant. In the wild it can grow to six feet, but grown indoors it will only reach two to three feet tall. The light green leaves are about the thickness of a thread and can get to a few inches long, growing on fleshy stems from a thick, hollow main stalk. Umbrella-shaped flower heads with tiny yellow flowers appear in the summer.

Dill is fairly easy to grow from seed. Follow the seed packet's instructions, and see page 67 for additional tips. Starter plants can also be purchased. Dill is an annual and will lose its vigor after flowering. For a continuous crop, plant seeds every few months through the year.

Light Requirements for Dill

Dill needs at least four hours of sun a day for best growth.

Watering Dill

Water once a week, and pour off any water remaining in the drainage saucer after 20 minutes.

Feeding Dill

Fertilize Dill every two to three weeks. Never use more fertilizer than the manufacturer recommends. See page 59 for more tips.

Pinching and Pruning Dill

Dill doesn't grow very well indoors, so pinching and pruning to control growth shouldn't be necessary. Remove the young flower heads if you want a longer harvest of leaves, but you'll sacrifice a crop of seeds.

Harvesting and Storing Dill

Dill leaves are best when used fresh. They can also be frozen. Cut leaves anytime and chop them finely for best flavor. Dill seeds can be used fresh or dried. Cut off faded flower stalks, place them in a paper bag and shake to separate the seeds. See page 79 for more on harvesting herbs.

OREGANO

Easy Care

Moderate

Bright, Full Sun

Perennial

Oregano is a sprawling plant with strong flavor. Needs frequent pinching to control growth. Regular division helps to maintain full flavor. Can be used fresh or dried.

Even the person with the most mild-mannered palate, who cringes at anything beyond salt and pepper, has probably developed a taste for Oregano. It's what gives pizza sauce, and other tomato-based dishes, that fabulous flavor — and what warm-blooded American doesn't eat pizza? It was little known in this country until the soldiers returned from Italy after World War II raving about its flavor. A little Oregano goes a long way, and caution is recommended in its use. A small plant will provide enough seasoning for the average family.

Oregano isn't the most attractive of the Kitchen Treasures. It's a very sprawling plant with an almost unkempt, weedy look. The many thin, trailing stems spread up from the soil and can reach over two feet tall. The dark green, oval leaves are no more than an inch long and slight hairy. Small purple, pink or white flowers will appear at the stem tips from summer through fall.

Small Oregano plants can be purchased, and this herb can also be grown from seed. Follow the seed packet instructions and turn to page 67 for more tips. Oregano is a perennial and will grow for many years, but can lose flavor as it gets older. Divide the plant every two or three years to help renew it and create new plants. Page 74 has more on dividing plants.

Light Requirements for Oregano

Oregano grows best in at least four hours of sun a day.

Watering Oregano

Water every seven to ten days. Pour off any water left in the drainage saucer after 20 minutes. Let the soil become fairly dry between waterings.

Feeding Oregano

Fertilize once every spring. Never use more plant food than the package recommends. Page 59 has more about fertilizer.

Pinching and Pruning Oregano

Begin pinching back the stems when they are six inches tall to encourage full growth. Trim stems regularly for a fuller, less rambling plant.

Harvesting and Storing Oregano

Oregano can be used fresh or dried. The flavor is best just after the flowers bloom. Cut stems back to the first set of leaves, and use leaves fresh or dry them. New shoots should appear for another harvest. Go to page 79 for tips on harvesting herbs.

THYME

Easy Care

Moderate

Bright, Full Sun

Perennial

Thyme is a compact shrub with a strong scent. Needs lots of sun. Annual pruning helps to maintain flavor. Can be used fresh or dried.

This is the stately patriarch of the Kitchen Treasures family. It has a rich scent that stimulates the appetite, and a rich history as well. The Sumerians documented medicinal uses for Thyme over 5,000 years ago. During the Middle Ages, it was believed to increase courage and was given to knights as they went into battle. Today, Thyme is one of the most popular herbs in European cooking, and is also believed to strengthen the immune system and help treat colds. So sprinkle a little Thyme into your chicken soup when your favorite knight or maiden has a case of the sniffles.

Thyme is a compact evergreen shrub with thin, woody stems. They are covered in gray-green, oval leaves no more than one-quarter to one-half inch long. Depending on the plant, small flowers in pink, purple, red or white will appear in the summer. There are two primary varieties of *Common Thyme*: *English broad-leaf* and *French summer* or *narrow-leaf.* These will grow six to twelve inches tall. *Lemon Thyme* has a strong lemon scent; its stems trail and it does not grow as tall as Common Thyme.

Thyme is slow to mature from seed, so it's best to buy starter plants. A perennial, it will grow for many years but will become woody and less flavorful if not pruned back in the spring.

Light Requirements for Thyme

Thyme does best in six to eight hours of sun each day.

Watering Thyme

Water every five to seven days, and test the soil with your finger periodically to be sure it's fairly moist. Pour off any water remaining in the drainage saucer after 20 minutes.

Feeding Thyme

Fertilize Thyme once in the spring. Never use more fertilizer than the package recommends. See page 59 for more on fertilizer.

Pinching and Pruning Thyme

Every spring, cut the plant back to half its size. This keeps the stems from getting woody and encourages bushy new growth.

Harvesting and Storing Thyme

Thyme can be used fresh, and it dries well. Harvest fresh leaves anytime after two inches of new growth has appeared. To dry, cut stems back to half of the season's growth, just before the flowers open, and follow the directions on page 81.

TARRAGON

Light Active Care

Wet

Moderate to Bright, Full Sun

Perennial

Tarragon is lush and attractive — one variety is cool-blue elegant while the other has bright sunny flowers. A fast growing perennial. Best used fresh.

This is probably the most mysterious and intriguing of the Kitchen Treasure herbs. A mainstay in French cooking, it's like a Parisian agent, with dusky-colored leaves and a complex flavor that's both sweet and tart — a subtle, musky combination of licorice and lemon. The leaves are high in Vitamins A and C.

There are two varieties of Tarragon used for cooking. *French Tarragon* grows two to three feet tall. It has dark, almost blue-green narrow leaves up to two inches long growing on soft, slender stems that spread out in all directions. The densely covered stems look like a blue velvet curtain. This plant must have cold temperatures in winter to grow well. You can put French Tarragon on a cold porch to die back until spring, or try *Winter Tarragon*. This plant has a different look and will grow well without cold weather. It's related to the common marigold, and in cooler weather has small yellow flowers with a single row of petals around a yellow tuft. Winter Tarragon grows one to two feet tall and has narrow green leaves.

Tarragon is best grown from starter plants. Both types are perennials, and should be divided every two to three years for better flavor and more vigorous growth. Turn to page 74 for more on dividing herbs.

Light Requirements for Tarragon

Tarragon prefers at least four hours of sun a day, but will tolerate moderate light.

Watering Tarragon

Water every five to seven days, and pour off any drainage water left in the saucer after 20 minutes. Check the soil regularly with your finger to make sure it's fairly moist.

Feeding Tarragon

Fertilize Tarragon once in the spring and once in summer. Never use more fertilizer than the package recommends. For more on fertilizer, turn to page 59.

Pinching and Pruning Tarragon

Tarragon can grow quickly. Cut back stems occasionally if you want to keep the plant's growth manageable.

Harvesting and Storing Tarragon

Tarragon is best used fresh; it dries well but loses some of its flavor. For fresh use, harvest leaves at any time. For drying, cut stems back to three inches in early summer and early fall. See page 79 for more on harvesting and drying herbs.

MINT

 Light Active Care

 Wet

 Moderate to Bright, Full Sun

 Perennial

Most popular varieties of Mint are Peppermint and Spearmint. Fast-growing. Needs lots of pinching to maintain appearance. Best used fresh, but can be dried.

Mint has many different uses, and it's a good thing, because it grows like crazy. It flavors cooling Mint juleps, and green jelly for roast lamb, and desserts, and Mediterranean foods, and... and.... Chewing a leaf will freshen your breath, and Peppermint will help to calm an upset stomach. Just about everyone likes Mint, except for mice. Hang mint stalks in your attic and the little critters will spend the winter at someone else's house.

The two most common varieties of Mint are *Spearmint* and *Peppermint*. In case you haven't had a stick of gum in your life, Spearmint has a rich, almost sweet flavor, while Peppermint has a sharper, almost peppery coolness. Spearmint grows one to three feet tall on firm stems. The round, pointed two-inch leaves are dark green with deep veins. Flower spikes with purple or pink blossoms appear in summer. Peppermint is a bit stockier, growing one to three feet tall with thinner, reddish stems. The leaves are narrow and pointed and grow to three inches, with a dark green, almost purplish hue. Both varieties grow quickly and need regular pinching to stay compact.

Grow Spearmint and Peppermint from starter plants. Mint spreads rapidly by underground running roots. Divide the plant every spring to keep it from choking the pot.

See page 74 for tips on dividing plants. A final word of caution: whenever you pinch or harvest mint, be careful not to get the leaf oil in your eye. That minty freshness feels good in your mouth, but is a little too zippy for the eyes.

Light Requirements for Mint
Mint prefers two to four hours of sun a day, but can also tolerate moderate light.

Watering Mint
Water every five to seven days. Pour off any water remaining in the drainage saucer after 20 minutes. Don't let the soil dry out. Check periodically with your finger to make sure it's moist.

Feeding Mint
Fertilize Mint every three to four weeks. Never use more fertilizer than recommended by the manufacturer. Page 59 has more about plant food.

Pinching and Pruning Mint
Pinch off new growth regularly to encourage fuller plants. If stems are long and lanky, cut plants back to a few inches tall. Pinch out flower stalks if you want to continue leaf growth.

Harvesting and Storing Mint

Mint can be used fresh or dried. Pick fresh leaves at any time. For drying, cut stems back to the first set of leaves, just before flowers begin to open. Leaves used after the plant flowers can have a harsh aroma and flavor. See page 79 for more about harvesting and storing.

MARJORAM

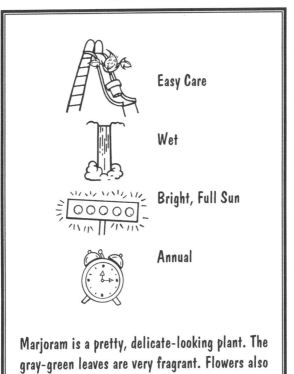

Easy Care

Wet

Bright, Full Sun

Annual

Marjoram is a pretty, delicate-looking plant. The gray-green leaves are very fragrant. Flowers also have a distinct flavor. Can be used fresh or dried.

This ancient herb symbolizes happiness and well-being both in the here and the hereafter, and is mentioned in books by the early Greeks, who recommended its use for women in childbirth as well as for funeral wreathes. Marjoram is related to Oregano, and has a similar appearance and flavor, but sweeter and milder. Marjoram oil is used as a perfume in soapmaking. Because Marjoram's flavor is delicate, it should be added to food just before serving for best results.

Marjoram is a bit of a rambling plant, but is not as freewheeling as its cousin, so it doesn't need constant pinching and pruning. It grows to a foot tall and spreads about the same distance. The many slender stems are covered in one-inch, grayish-green leaves that are oval and a bit furry. Tiny, light pink flowers appear in summer. The flowers have a sweet and spicy flavor, and can be used in cooking.

Marjoram is best treated as an annual. Buy starter plants, or grow from seed, so you can plant some every few months to have a non-stop harvest. Check instructions on the seed packet, and see page 67 for more tips.

Light Requirements for Marjoram
Marjoram prefers at least four hours a day of full sun.

Watering Marjoram

Water every five to seven days, and pour off any water remaining in the drainage saucer after 20 minutes. Check the soil with your finger every few days to make sure it's barely moist.

Feeding Marjoram

Fertilize once after the plants are several inches tall. Never use more fertilizer than the manufacturer recommends. Page 59 has more fertilizer tips.

Pinching and Pruning Marjoram

Pinch off stem tips periodically for fuller growth. To lengthen the harvest season for leaves, pinch off the flower buds as they appear.

Harvesting and Storing Marjoram

Marjoram leaves can be used fresh, and also dry well; flavor increases when dried. Pick leaves and stem tips anytime for fresh use. To dry, cut stems back to the first set of leaves after the flowers bloom. New shoots will appear for one or two more harvests. See page 79 for more tips.

PARSLEY

Very Easy Care

Moderate

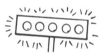
Bright, Full Sun

Annual

Parsley is an airy, upright plant that does well in pots. Two varieties have different appearance, different flavors. Harvest regularly to encourage growth. Best used fresh, but can also be frozen.

Parsley has been given credit since ancient times for health, strength and even the ability to protect against drunkenness, although I haven't seen that reported in the medical journals.

It's possible that Parsley suffers from overexposure by one-star (and no-star) restaurants. Poor Parsley! It's been strewn about as a garnish for so long that people don't really take it seriously. But Parsley is actually a very flavorful herb that can brighten up the taste of many foods. In fact, if you have onions on your burger and eat the frilly Parsley sprig garnish, it will help to clear up your breath! Once you start growing Parsley and using it regularly, you may find that you need more plants.

There are several varieties of Parsley. The most familiar is *Curly Parsley*, the ornamental, curly-leaf variety. It has a very sharp, almost spicy flavor. *Italian* or *Flat-Leaf Parsley* is preferred by many cooks; the flavor is more intense than the curly type. It's not sharper, but earthier, richer. Both varieties send up their leaves on ribbed stems that grow in a tuft from a central base. The plants can grow eight to twelve inches tall with a similar spread. Curly Parsley leaves are a bright green, while the flat-leafed variety is a darker green.

Parsley can be grown from seeds, but they take some time to sprout. Give it a try, following the package directions, or just purchase starter plants. Plants will last two years, but tend to get bitter in the second season. It's better to treat them as an annual.

Light Requirements for Parsley
For best growth, Parsley prefers at least four hours of sun a day.

Watering Parsley
Water once a week, and pour off any water remaining in the drainage saucer after 20 minutes.

Feeding Parsley
Fertilize every two to three weeks. Never use more fertilizer than the manufacturer recommends. See page 59 for more on fertilizing plants.

Pinching and Pruning Parsley
Parsley doesn't branch, so it won't benefit from pinching and pruning. Harvest stems regularly to encourage new growth.

Harvesting and Storing Parsley

You can harvest Parsley leaves at any time, once plants are six inches tall. New leaves won't grow on a stem, so clip the stem down to the plant's base and trim off the leaves. Dried Parsley doesn't really resemble fresh Parsley, but the fresh herb can be frozen. Turn to page 79 for more on harvesting and storing herbs.

CILANTRO

  Very Easy Care

 Moderate

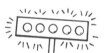 Bright, Full Sun

  Annual

The richly flavored leaves of this frilly plant are called Cilantro (and sometimes fresh Coriander), and the seeds are called Coriander. Leaves are best used fresh. Seeds can be harvested and dried.

Cilantro leaves, sometimes called *fresh Coriander*, are very popular in Latin cooking. They have been used in Asian cooking since ancient times, and are sometimes called *Chinese Parsley*. Cilantro has a very musky, pungent flavor like a mixture of sage and lemon. The plant's seeds are known as *Coriander*, and have a lemony flavor with an aroma of orange and anise. They are used in many cuisines. Coriander has been cultivated for over 3,000 years and has been used in love potions and to attain immortality. If you aspire to be an immortal lover, or if you just wish to flavor foods, let some of your Cilantro plants go to seed.

This plant has delicately branched stems that grow one to two feet tall. The leaves are dark green, frilly sprigs a few inches long. The plant looks very similar to Italian Parsley. In summer it sends up small, lacy flower heads that have tiny white, pink or lavender blossoms and are very pretty.

Cilantro is an annual and is best grown from starter plants. The plants will last longer if you pinch out the flower stalks. Consider growing a few plants for Cilantro leaves and a few for Coriander seeds.

Light Requirements for Cilantro

Cilantro needs at least four hours of sun a day for best growth.

Watering Cilantro

Water once a week, and pour off any water remaining in the drainage saucer after 20 minutes.

Feeding Cilantro

Fertilize every two to three weeks. Never use more fertilizer than the manufacturer recommends. See page 59 for more about fertilizing plants.

Pinching and Pruning Cilantro

Pinch growing tips periodically to encourage fuller growth. To lengthen leaf harvest, pinch out flower stalks as they appear.

Harvesting and Storing Cilantro

Cilantro leaves are best used fresh, and can be harvested any time after the plant reaches six inches tall. To harvest the Coriander seeds, cut the flowering stalks after the seed pods have turned brown and hang them in a paper bag to dry. Shake the stalks to release the pods, and then rub the pods between your hands to open them and release the seeds. For more about harvesting herbs, go to page 79.

HOW TO CHOOSE
AN HERB PLANT

It Takes Commitment and Good Taste

Buying an herb plant to grow indoors is pretty much like buying any other house-plant. You want to be sure your home has the right conditions to help your herb grow, and that you have enough energy and com-mitment to provide the care it needs. If you're a member of the jet set and spend weeks on the Riviera, your go-go life prob-ably won't allow you to water Tarragon every few days. If you've only got one win-dow that gets a few hours of sun each day, you're going to have to pass on that sun-lov-ing Sage. And if you haven't got the time for Thyme, there's no sense buying it.

THE TEST OF THYME

1. Do you like the taste of Thyme? Do you use it often in cooking?

2. Do you have enough light for it? Do you have time to water it weekly?

3. Does the Thyme plant look healthy? Is the soil moist and loose?

4. Does the plant have a reasonable price?

Flavor is the first order of business. Think about what flavors you like and the types of food you cook. If you're one of the seven people in America who doesn't like pizza because you can't stand the taste of Oregano, then don't have it sprawling across your windowsill. Do you buy pickled pigs feet because they look cute in the 'fridge even though you'd never even open the jar to taste them? I don't think so.

Looks Aren't Everything

True, your herbs will look nice and add a touch of lively green to your home. But unlike other houseplants, you're not buying them just for their looks. Think taste first, then care issues, then appearance. If you love the flavor and aroma of Rosemary and have the right conditions to grow it, but you think that it looks like a mountain of needles, ask yourself if you're willing to put up with the plant's appearance for the flavor. You might end up adoring that spiky plant.

A Healthy Herb Is a Tasty Herb

Once you've decided on a type of herb to buy, choose one that's in good shape. You wouldn't buy bruised apples or yellow broccoli. Look for plants that have a nice shape and are evenly covered with leaves. Avoid those with wilted or yellow leaves, browning tips or straggly stems. Basically, choose a plant that looks strong and attractive. You don't want to be cooking with herbs from an unhealthy plant, and harvesting leaves from a straggly plant isn't going to make it look any better.

Make sure the herb has good taste, too. No, not in music and art — I'm talking flavor! Nibble a leaf or rub it between your fingers to smell the scent. If it doesn't have a rich taste and aroma, it may be divided from an old plant or just may not be from good stock. Remember, it's for cooking; don't buy one that's shy with its flavor.

Buying quality houseplants requires a few other diagnostic tests. Make sure the soil feels moist and fairly loose in the pot. If it feels dry or hard, has mossy mildew, or you can see roots at the top, look at another plant. Check the holes at the bottom of the pot. If you can see thick roots or roots are sticking out, it needs repotting; pass it by. Finally, if the plants in a store don't seem healthy or well cared for, take your business elsewhere.

You Want How Much for This?

You don't have to spend a lot for an herb plant. If you really want to go cheap, buy seeds. They're only about a dollar a packet, and you'll experience the joy of germination. Do keep in mind, however, that some herbs are difficult to grow from seed, and a few will take two years before the plants reach maturity.

If you'd prefer immediate gratification, buy starter plants. Because herbs are a food plant, you're more likely to find them in better grocery stores, while they may not be as common in discount stores that carry only indoor houseplants. Of course they're available at garden centers. Herbs are usually sold in four-inch pots and can cost anywhere from a few dollars to almost ten dollars. The difference is where you purchase the plant. A small pot of Dill may cost $2.99 at a nursery. At a gourmet market the same plant may cost $4.99, while a florist may charge $7.99. Shopping for herbs is no different from shopping for anything else — you want the best quality at the lowest price.

MORE ABOUT CARE OF HERBS

Water

Everyday Chemistry

Who would think that little molecules of hydrogen and oxygen would be so important? But H_2O, or "water" if you're on familiar terms, is one of the essential building blocks of life. It keeps us alive, and it keeps plants alive. Water is a plant's lifeblood, carrying nutrients from the roots all the way out to the leaf tips and flowers.

The human body is made mostly of water, and the same can be said for plants. Those dried herbs in the little jars are all dark and crispy because the water is gone. Because water is so vital to plant health, it's important that you give plants the right amount. Too little or too much water can both lead to problems, although overwatering causes more damage. Please don't think that underwatering your Sage until it shrivels up is a convenient drying process. It doesn't work that way.

Watering herbs is simple. All you need to know is how to water them and when to water them. Once you get these concepts, you're halfway toward harvesting your first crop of Tarragon.

How to Water

Try this: On a hot day, stand outside in the sun for a few hours. See if you can make it the whole day. When you come in, sweaty and thirsty, take two tablespoons of water. Will your thirst be quenched? Hardly. Herbs sit in the sun for a good part of every day, and they only get a drink about once a week! Don't just give them a dribble of water.

Water your plants so they get that same refreshing "ahh" feeling that you get drinking a big cold glass. Remember, the roots need to take up enough for the whole plant. Pour water over the soil until it comes out of the pot's drainage holes. Be sure to have a saucer or something underneath to catch the drainage. Trust me on this last point. Or if you want to learn the hard way, you can. You'll only make that mistake once.

Check the plant after 20 minutes. If there's any water left in the drainage saucer, pour it out. By this time, the soil and roots have absorbed as much as they can. If the soil gets waterlogged, the roots can rot.

Cheap Water Grows Fine Herbs

You don't need to douse your Dill with pricey bottled water; tap water is fine. Just make sure it's pleasantly warm so the plants can take it up easily. Cold water can shock plants, and with some of the magic powers of these herbs, you don't want to get on their bad side. Water that tastes or smells strongly of chlorine should be left in an open container overnight to let it evaporate. Water softeners use chemicals that can damage plants, so use cheap bottled water, the kind in the gallon jug.

And Another Thing

It's important to provide any plant with enough water to stay happy. But there's an additional reason to make sure your herbs are well watered. Their flavor comes from oils in the leaves. If a plant doesn't get enough water, the oils can become overly pungent or bitter, affecting the taste of the herb. So water your herbs freely, just not enough to drown them.

When to Water

Most culinary wizards have that special "cooking sense" to know when something's done. I can stare at a roast until my eyes glaze and I still won't be able to tell if it should come out of the oven. To know when to water your herbs, you have to "read" them like a roast, because essentially you water a plant when it needs water.

Think of your finger as a meat thermometer. Stick your finger into the soil about an inch. If it feels fairly moist, it's probably okay. If it's dry, it's time to water. If the leaves look droopy or feel limp, the plant's thirsty. Very thirsty.

Because most herbs spend a good deal of time in direct sun, you may need to check them frequently to make sure the soil hasn't dried out. The plant descriptions in this book provide guidelines for watering your herbs. The plant's container, soil and the conditions of the room may change the watering requirements for your plants.

Light

You Are My Sunshine

How many plants grow in the dark? In case you haven't been in a lot of caves, I'll answer that for you: besides mushrooms, not many. (They're a fungus, so they don't

RECIPES FOR DISASTER

Watch for these signs of underwatering or overwatering, and adjust your main ingredient — water — as appropriate.

Dry, Underwatered and Overcooked	Soggy, Overwatered and Undercooked
• Growth slows	• Leaves get soft, rotten patches
• Leaves wilt or become limp	• Leaves curl, yellow and tips turn brown
• Lower leaves curl, yellow or fall off	• Young and old leaves fall off
• Leaf edges turn brown and dry	• Leaf growth is poor

really count.) Light is not something that keeps plants warm and happy; it's a source of food.

If you paid attention in science class, you remember something called photosynthesis. You probably forgot the details right after the test. Don't worry, you don't need to relearn the process to grow herbs. But understanding that a plant uses photosynthesis to turn light into carbohydrates will help you realize how important light is.

All plants need the right amount of light to grow properly. Not enough light can make a plant spindly and stunted. Too much can turn leaves pale or even burn them. You shouldn't have to worry about giving your herbs too much light, since most of them require hours of full sun each day. The key is finding a place in your house that gets long periods of direct sunlight. If you live in a greenhouse, your lighting concerns are over. If you're like most of us, you'll probably need to put your herbs on a sunny windowsill.

Plants need light, so they grow toward it, kind of the way you might be drawn to

SEARCHING FOR THE SUN

The best light conditions for herbs are in a south-facing window, because it gets sun for the longest period of time. East- and west-facing windows are the next best places to park your herbs. Check a window for a day and see how long the sun hits it. A north-facing window gets little if any direct sun, so don't even try.

THERE'S MORE THAN LIGHT AT THE WINDOW

Even though your herbs will probably be on a windowsill, be careful that the leaves don't touch the glass. They could get burned in hot summer heat, or frozen in winter. (No, this isn't a good way to freeze your herbs.) Even if the leaves aren't touching the glass, plants on a windowsill can be shocked by cold winter drafts, so make sure your special herb window is well-insulated.

that frozen yogurt place at the mall. Rotate your plants occasionally to help them grow evenly. You don't need to set them on a battery-powered Lazy Susan. Just give them a quarter- or half-turn every few days, once a week, sometimes longer. It depends on how quickly the plant grows. If it's practically lying on its side, it's definitely time.

Fertilizer

Everybody Needs Good Nutrition

These days we all watch what we eat. We make sure our diets include lots of carbohydrates and fresh fruits and veggies. We take vitamins and eat sports bars when we're exercising. Putting the right things into our bodies keeps us in optimum shape. To keep your herbs in great shape, give them a little energy bar in the form of fertilizer. If you enjoy cooking with fresh herbs, you're going to want your plants to be as big as they can get.

The Numbers Game

Plant food is made up of three basic minerals: nitrogen (for active growth), phosphate (for strong roots) and potassium (for healthy leaves and flowers). The best fertilizer for most plants has a balanced blend of minerals. This is listed on the package by three identical numbers such as 10-10-10.

If you're growing an herb for its leaves, use a fertilizer that's a bit higher in nitrogen, which might be a 20-10-10 blend. Nitrogen supports foliage growth, sort of the way Vitamin A is good for the eyes. If you're growing Dill for the seeds, cut back on the nitrogen with a 5-10-10 fertilizer. There are many different plant food blends, such as a 17-10-5. Just look for the ratio of the numbers, and don't be afraid to ask the nursery staff for help. They love talking about this stuff. If they get really technical, just nod pleasantly and visualize world peace until they stop.

Many Flavors to Grow Your Flavorings

Plant food comes in many different

forms. Liquids and powders are mixed with water so that you can give plants a snack when they need it. This is probably the best approach for herbs, since mixing up batches of fertilizer gives you a little more control over feeding time. Time-release pellets and sticks go into the soil and release fertilizer with each watering. Even though the time-release forms provide a weak solution, the continual feeding may be too much for herbs. You want them to taste fresh and natural, not like they've been on steroids. And speaking of natural, fish emulsion (which is what it sounds like) is a natural fertilizer that's mixed in water, and is another good option for an herbal snack.

You'll find fertilizer at plant, discount and hardware stores. Even though herbs are often grown outdoors, don't use fertilizer for gardens. Outdoor growing conditions are very different from the conditions in a little pot on the windowsill.

The Perils of Overeating

All of us have gorged ourselves from time to time. Whether it's a fantastic spread of specialty dishes from around the world, or a half-gallon of Mint chocolate chip ice cream, it's fun and satisfying. That is until it's over. Then we deal with that bloated feeling,

heartburn or indigestion. And we think, "Never again," until the next big buffet.

Plants can also feel lousy from gorging on food, only the effects may be more harmful. Too much fertilizer can burn a plant's roots and leaves. Since you control their diet, mix fertilizer solutions at one-half or even one-quarter of the recommended strength. Also be aware of each herb's individual needs. Some plants like to nibble every few weeks, while others only need a hearty meal once a year.

Pinching and Pruning

You Gotta Give Some to Get Some

It may seem illogical, but in order to get a plant to grow lush and full, you often need to remove some of it. Mother Nature has built some marvelous restorative powers into living organisms. If a starfish loses an arm, it will grow it back. Now imagine if, instead of growing one arm back, the starfish grew back two, or four or even six arms!

That's the principle with pinching and pruning plants. Pinching the tip off a Mint

> ## Z-z-z-z-z-z-z
> Whether plants are grown indoors or out, most follow the seasons. They grow actively in spring and summer, and go into a low-growth or dormant period during fall and winter. Let plants take a snooze during this period. Avoid fertilizing them from October to March, and go easy on the water. Just be careful in homes with very dry winter heat; these conditions may require a little more water for the plants.

stem will cause it to grow two stems where it was removed. Pruning back half the year's growth on a Rosemary shrub will force it to send out a mass of new growth that's more vigorous, fresh and flavorful. Plants are compelled to grow; pinching and pruning just inspires them to grow stronger. You might not be happy with the immediate results, especially when you've cut that Rosemary from ten inches down to four inches. But after a few weeks, new shoots will sprout and the plant will be rejuvenated.

Pinching

Pinching is done on plants that branch, like Basil, Mint and Oregano. Left on their own, the stems will just keep growing up and up and up. Without pinching, you'd have six very tall branches. Pinching stems back causes them to branch, creating a plant with more leaves and denser growth. With your fingernails, simply remove about an inch of young branch tips, right down to where a leaf begins. Some plants will send out two new shoots where the tip was removed. Other plants may send out more new growth where older leaves join the branch.

How much pinching you do depends on how bushy you want the plant, and on how

A CLEAN HERB IS A HAPPY HERB

Plants are living things, so they also breathe. If their leaves are covered in dust, it's like having a head cold. To keep your plants clean and breathing freely, give them a light shower. You can do this with the kitchen sink sprayer or the bathroom shower — just don't use the massage setting. Make sure the water is pleasantly warm, like a spring rain. Be sure to wash "behind the ears" by wetting both sides of the leaves. Showers will keep your plants fresh, and can also replace a usual watering.

quickly it grows. Mint grows very fast; you could pinch it back every few weeks. Slower growing plants may only need pinching once or twice a year. It's best to pinch plants while they're actively growing, so they can put energy into new growth.

Pruning

Pruning is like an advanced version of pinching, because you're removing more than just the young tips. You might prune a plant to cut away straggly, older or unhealthy branches. Or to encourage a new season of fresh growth or keep it small to fit in its space.

For a bushy plant like Basil, you may do some occasional selective pruning. If a branch looks weak or is growing in a strange direction, just cut it off cleanly with sharp scissors to the main stem. This type of pruning helps keep a plant strong, since the plant will direct energy to a weak section. It also makes a more attractive plant. Prune when the plant is actively growing, and as long as the leaves are healthy, cook 'em up!

For sprawling and shrub-type plants, the pruning technique is more like clipping a hedge. With Rosemary and Thyme, just cut the stems back in the spring, like giving the plant a flat-top. This will force the plant to send up new young growth that will be

more vigorous and flavorful and less woody. With a sprawling plant like Oregano, you may also want to just cut all the stems into submission. This can be done any time while the plant is actively growing — even several times — and will help it stay compact and bushy. Don't let prunings go to waste, but with older, woody growth, it may be better to dry the cuttings than use them fresh. See page 81 for more on drying herbs.

Don't be afraid of heavy pruning; new growth will appear. Remember that a haircut always looks better after a week or two. (Unless you paid six bucks for it.) If you like, save some of the healthier prunings to propagate into new plants. See page 73 for tips.

Planting Seeds and Repotting

The Seed of Life

Unlike most houseplants, some herbs can be grown from seed. If you're like me and have never won an award for patience, you can pass on the "seed experience" and buy herbs that are already alive and kicking in their own pots. If, however, you want to live the miracle of watching a small seed grow into a mature and tasty plant, pick up a packet of seeds at your local garden or discount store. Remember that some herb seeds are used for cooking. These aren't cured for planting, so don't buy a jar of Dill seed at the grocery store and expect it to be fruitful and multiply. About all it will do is make a good batch of mustard pickles.

To plant herbs from seed, fill a two- to four-inch pot with commercial potting soil. Don't fill it to the rim; leave some room for water to drain. Follow the instructions on the seed packet for how deep to plant the seeds. You really only want one plant in a small pot, but plant more than one seed. There's no guarantee that a solitary seed will sprout.

Once the seeds are planted, water the soil carefully! You didn't gently pat the soil over the seeds just to deluge them with a tidal wave. Keep the soil moist to help the seeds sprout. At this stage, don't put the pot in direct sun, which can quickly dry the top layer of soil. You may want to cover the pot with plastic wrap secured with an elastic band to help retain moisture. Once the seeds sprout, remove the wrap.

Playing Darwin

If all goes well (and it should), you'll have a handful of little baby herb seedlings in the pot. Make sure the soil is moist, watering it about every day or two. The young root will be short and tiny, and a seedling can wither and die quickly in dry soil. Once the seedlings can be seen, you can move the pot to a sunny spot, but limit the amount of sun for at least a couple of weeks. It's easy for a tiny seedling to burn up in a few hours of hot sun.

After the seedlings have developed a second set of leaves, pull out the seedlings that look weak. This is nothing more than Darwin's theory of "survival of the fittest;" you're just hastening the process. Leave just one or two strong, hearty seedlings in the pot, and thank the others for their effort as you toss them in the garbage. Make sure the plants you keep are near the center of the pot; a hearty specimen that's sprouting at the pot's rim is going to be maladjusted and will always be living life on the edge.

Move 'Em On Out

For herbs that are annuals, don't repot, just start with new plants when they get tired. But perennial herbs can outgrow their pots. Others need to be divided and repotted to keep them vigorous. (Page 74 has more information on dividing plants.) Repotting plants gives you the chance to get down and dirty. Think about whipping up a dessert and getting covered in flour and butter. (Oh, that doesn't happen to you?) Anyway, instead of being dusted in white flour, you'll be covered in black dirt! Use the opportunity to relive those childhood

ONLY THE STRONG SURVIVE

| These guys will compete for space and food as they mature, and none of them will be the best they can be. | These two strong plants probably would have overpowered the others anyway. Now they can thrive from the beginning. |

memories. Make yourself a mud pie or two for old times' sake.

Repotting a plant into a larger pot provides nutrients from fresh soil and lets the roots grow. You can tell a plant needs repotting if the soil dries out quickly between waterings. If roots are coming out of the pot's drainage holes or you can see that they're the size of parsnips, the plant is pot-bound, which means its little feet are very cramped. Either way, it's time to put down some newspaper and get dirty. It's best to repot in the early spring to help the plant start a season of healthy growth.

First Get a Pot and Some Soil

Choose a new pot that's one to two inches wider at the rim than the current pot. If you go from a four-inch to a ten-inch pot, the plant will look like a twig on the prairie, and you'll be looking at a lot of dirt. Be sure the pot has drainage holes, or you'll increase the risk of overwatering. Finally, use a good commercial potting

commercial potting soil: a mixture of decomposed vegetable matter, wood fiber and vermiculite (silicate material that helps the soil drain), sold in 5-, 10- and 25-lb. bags by groceries, nurseries and other retailers

soil; it's pasteurized to kill organisms that could harm your plants. Avoid using outdoor garden soil. It's filled with little bugs and things that should stay outdoors.

Water the plant about an hour before you repot it. This helps keep the soil together and lessens the shock factor. When you're ready to take the plant out of its pot, use a little tenderness and common sense. It's been living there for a year or more; you wouldn't want to be yanked out of your home, would you? Spread your fingers over the soil with the plant between them, tip the pot upside down and tap it on the edge of a counter. The plant should fall into your hand. Keep tapping and lightly wiggling the plant until it comes free.

Once the plant's free, put a little soil in the new pot and set the plant in. The plant's base should sit about an inch lower than the pot's rim to keep water from pouring off. Adjust the soil level if necessary. Once the plant's at the right level, add soil evenly all around it. Use a chopstick or screwdriver to fit soil into tight spaces and avoid air pockets. Put some fresh soil over the existing soil, but don't bury the plant's base. Press the plant firmly into the pot; but don't jam it in. If the soil's packed too tightly, water won't penetrate, and you'll have to pot it again.

Give the plant a good drink of water, but don't fertilize for about a month to let the plant adjust to the shock of moving. If the herb needs regular fertilizing, keep feeding it after the first dose of fertilizer. If it only needs one snack a year, consider it fed.

Propagating

The Wonders of Creation

Propagating plants means creating new plants from mature ones. Sometimes this means taking a little piece of a plant, getting it to grow new roots and nurturing it to become a full-grown plant. Other times it means hacking an overgrown plant into chunks with a big sharp knife and putting them in pots. Either way, it's a fascinating and fulfilling process. In more scientific terms, these two techniques are known as stem cutting and root division. These are both common approaches for propagating many types of houseplants. But for some herbs, division not only increases the number of plants, but is necessary to rejuvenate older plants.

1. Stem Cuttings

To propagate from stem cuttings, choose

a healthy, growing stem. Cut the tip off cleanly with sharp scissors; bruised ends may not root. Carefully remove leaves from a few inches of stem above the cut, so they won't be under water or soil when rooting.

Put the stem in soil to sprout roots. Cuttings from some herbs will also root in water. If you root directly in soil, you can dust the stem end with rooting hormone powder, which can be found at any good garden shop. This will help roots form faster, but isn't necessary. Keep the soil moist so the new roots don't dry out. Stems rooting in water can be put into pots when about two inches of root have developed.

> rooting hormone powder: found at plant stores and nurseries, this powder accelerates root growth in plant cuttings rooting in soil

2. Root Division

This method creates new plants and rejuvenates older ones by dividing up the plant and root mass. Take the plant out of its pot and examine the plant's base and roots. There may be distinct sections that can be easily separated, or you may just need to cut the plant in equal pieces. Place a large carving knife at the top of the soil. Press down and rock the knife to make a clean cut through the plant base and roots. Don't saw the roots; this will bruise them. Pot the sections, and discard any that look weak or spent.

Propagating Basil. Basil can be propagated from stem cuttings. Put cuttings in water and pot when roots develop. Or root cuttings directly in soil, keeping it moist to help roots grow.

Propagating Sage. Sage can become tired after four or five years, so divide it every few years in early spring. Take the plant out of its pot, cut the plant and root mass into sections with a sharp knife, and pot each section separately. In summer, Sage can be propagated from younger stem cuttings. Put cuttings in water and pot when roots develop. Or root cuttings directly in soil, keeping it moist to help roots grow.

Propagating Rosemary. Propagate by putting cuttings directly in soil, keeping it moist to help roots grow. Pot several cuttings together for a fuller plant. Rosemary doesn't root well in water.

Propagating Chives. Chives should be divided in the early spring. To separate sections of the plant, pull the roots apart with your fingers or use a knife, and pot the sections.

Propagating Oregano. Oregano should be divided at least every two or three years to keep it healthy and flavorful. In the early spring or fall, cut the plant and root mass into sections with a sharp knife and pot each section separately. If you divide Oregano in the fall, don't fertilize it until the following spring.

Propagating Thyme. Thyme can be divided in early spring. Remove the plant from its pot, cut the plant and root mass into sections with a sharp knife, and pot each section separately. Thyme can also be propagated from stem cuttings. Put cuttings directly in soil, keeping it moist to help roots grow. Or place cuttings in water and plant after the roots have developed.

Propagating Tarragon. This plant can be propagated by dividing it in early spring. Use a sharp knife to cut the plant and root mass into sections, and pot each section separately. Tarragon should be divided at least every three years to keep it vigorous.

Propagating Mint. Mint is easily propagated from stem cuttings. Put cuttings in water and pot when roots develop. Or root cuttings directly in soil, keeping it moist to help roots grow. Mint can and should be divided in early spring because the running roots can quickly fill a pot. Take the plant out of its pot and cut sections of the plant and the roots. Plant each section separately.

Propagating Marjoram. Propagate Marjoram by using healthy, mature cuttings. Put cuttings in water and pot in soil when roots have developed. Or root cuttings directly in soil. Be sure to keep the soil moist, since Marjoram cuttings are so small.

A GIFT IN GOOD TASTE!

One benefit of propagating plants is that they make great, inexpensive gifts. Tie a ribbon around a small pot of propagated Rosemary, attach a recipe for roasted chicken, and you've got a welcome present.

Propagating Dill, Parsley and Cilantro. These herbs are annuals and cannot be propagated by cuttings or division.

Take Good Care of the Babies

Avoid fertilizing plants propagated from cuttings for at least several months. It's easy to overfertilize and burn the young roots. Once the plant seems established and has been actively growing for a little while, you can give it a weak dose of fertilizer then slowly build up to regular feedings. For divided plants that need only one shot of food at the start of the growing season, wait about a month after dividing them in the early spring.

Have patience when propagating plants. It can take anywhere from three to six weeks for a cutting to develop roots, and then it will slowly begin life as a growing, independent plant. Divisions are a little quicker on the uptake, but they also need time to adjust; they've just been chopped away!

HARVESTING AND STORING HERBS

Have Your Herbs and Eat Them, Too!

You know you've got a good thing going when you're growing plants that need to be harvested. Pretty as they may be, you can't do the same with foliage or flowering houseplants. You certainly can't eat them or cook with them! So next time someone raves about his eight-foot Ficus Tree, ask him if he's ever grabbed a few fresh Marjoram leaves off his windowsill and tossed them into a cassoulet. That should keep him quiet, and he probably won't even know what a cassoulet is.

Harvesting fresh herbs can be as simple as snipping off a few leaves as you need them, or drying flower heads to get the seeds. You don't need to wait for "harvest time" if you just want a few leaves for a sauce. Make sure they're fairly mature so they have full flavor, and use leaves that look healthy. Give them a quick rinse to remove any dust or debris and pat them dry with a towel before using them.

Never harvest more than half the leaves off a plant at one time. Leaves aren't just decoration; they keep a plant alive by taking in air and light. Be careful not to injure the stems when you remove leaves. Also keep in mind that an herb plant should look nice in your window, so remove leaves strategically. Don't pluck them all from one side so the plant looks like it fell into an electric fan. On plants with tall, woody stems like Rosemary and Thyme, pick leaves from different spots on the plant, or snip off a few stems and strip the leaves off. This helps to avoid skinny bare stems, which won't grow new leaves.

And Now for Some Serious Reapin'

Growing herbs like Dill and Cilantro for the seeds can really be considered harvesting. The flowers need to mature and go to seed, so there's a "season" to wait for. Then there's all that separating the wheat from the chaff business. Best of all, it's fun!

A few weeks after the flowers have faded, cut the stalks and hang them upside down in a warm, dark, dry place, ideally with good air circulation. This will help the flowers to continue drying. Put a paper bag over the flower heads to catch the seeds as they fall. After a couple of weeks, shake the bag to loosen all of the seeds, and throw away the dried stems. Dill seeds are fine right out of the bag. Coriander seeds have a pod-like hull around them. Briskly rub the pods between your hands to break them open and release the seeds.

Store your well-earned harvest in an airtight jar in a dark place. The seeds should retain their flavor for several years.

Harvesting for the Long Haul

Drying fresh herbs allows you to keep a convenient supply on hand, and is much more economical than purchasing dried herbs.

To dry leaves on the stem, wash the leaves and pat them dry with a towel. Then tie the stems together and hang the bunch upside down in a warm, dark place with good air circulation. When the leaves have

---

IF YOU LIKE NEWFANGLED GADGETS

Think that air-drying your herbs is too time-consuming, messy or just not in touch with the modern age? Dry them in the microwave. Just wash and dry two cups of loosely packed leaves and spread them evenly on two sheets of paper towel. Don't cover them. Cook at high power for two minutes. Check and keep cooking at 30-second intervals until the herbs are dried. This method preserves the leaves' color and flavor better than air drying. Personally, I think this takes a lot of the romance out of the process. Then again, I'm not too romantic when I feel like having a baked potato in minutes.

---

dried, strip them from the stems. You can also strip the leaves fresh and place them on a raised screen or rack to dry. Make sure it's in a dark, warm, airy spot.

Store dried leaves in an airtight container, preferably away from light. The flavor should last about a year.

It's a Little Dry for My Taste

Some herbs don't dry well; they lose their flavor. Parsley, Cilantro, Basil, Dill and Chives can be frozen. Wash the leaves, pat them dry and wrap them tightly in a plastic bag. Put enough in each bag for one use; it's hard to separate frozen herbs. They'll thaw into a mushy texture, so it's best to chop the herbs before you freeze them (you can use a food processor), or do it while they're still frozen. Don't plan on using them raw in a salad, but the flavor will still be great for cooking.

HERBS ON ICE

Freeze fresh Parsley and Basil in ice cube trays. Remove the leaves from the stems, wash and pat them dry, and chop them by hand or with a food processor. Add a little olive oil to make a paste, and spoon the mixture into the ice cube trays. Transfer the frozen cubes to a plastic bag. Toss a cube or two into sauce, stew or soup for a fresh taste!

CONTAINERS; DECORATING TIPS

Doesn't That Look Pretty?

Herbs are attractive plants, but they don't offer as many decorating options as other indoor plants because they need to be in direct sunlight. But just because your plants will be limited to a window area doesn't mean you can't be creative with how they look.

While herbs are usually sold in plain plastic pots, you can use more attractive pots made of clay, glazed ceramic or designer plastic. Make sure the pots have drainage holes; you don't want to risk overwatering. Herbs look great in unglazed terra cotta pots, but be aware that the clay absorbs water from the soil and allows the moisture to evaporate more quickly, so be prepared to water your plants more often.

Plan a Sit-In, or Just Hang Out

Plants in a window aren't required to sit on the windowsill. You can put some herbs in hanging pots to hang them in the sunlight. Slings to hold pots and hardware for hanging them are available in garden, hardware and discount stores. Combine a few hanging pots of herbs with several on the windowsill and you'll have an aromatic wall of green. If you discover that you're really into growing herbs indoors, you can knock out a window and put in one of those mini-greenhouse window attachments.

How Does Your Garden Grow?

If you've got a fairly deep windowsill, consider an herb dish garden. Fill a large container with soil and place a variety of plants together in it. Combine Rosemary, Thyme, Sage and Oregano for a Mediterranean garden. You can close your eyes, run the tap, breathe in the delightful blend of aromas and pretend you're cruising off the coast of Greece. Or make a dish garden of Italian, Lemon and Thai Basil. The different textures and colors of leaves in a dish garden will be like a painting done in foliage. Just remember when you're planting, don't completely fill the container with plants; they need room to grow!

Summering on the Deck

If you like, you can move your potted herbs out onto a sunny porch or deck in warmer months. Make sure the nights aren't too cold when you first put them out; they're accustomed to fairly consistent indoor temperatures. Bring them back in

when the weather gets cool in the fall, but check for insects. The flavorful oils in herbs tend to make them resistant to pests and disease, but plants kept outdoors can get aphids, spider mites or whiteflies. Aphids are little green or white bugs that suck the sap out of stems; just pick off any affected parts. Spider mites are hard to see, but do leave little webs on the leaves and suck the leaves dry so they curl. Whiteflies are tiny, moth-like bugs that suck sap and excrete a sticky substance. Mites and whiteflies are hard to get rid of; you may want to toss the plant and start again.

• • •

There's no substitute for the taste and smell of fresh herbs. You'll benefit from having them in your food, and you'll even benefit from having a little family of green, aromatic friends sitting on your windowsill. Try it; you'll see.

BIBLIOGRAPHY

Brennan, Georgeanne and Luebbermann, Mimi. *Little Herb Gardens*. San Francisco, CA: Chronicle Books, 1993.

Frontier Herbs. World Wide Web. Norway, IA: Frontier Cooperative Herbs, 1996.

Herbs, An Illustrated Guide. Menlo Park, CA: Sunset Publishing Corporation, 1972.

Martha Stewart Living. New York: Omnimedia, March 1997.

Morash, Marian. *The Victory Garden Cookbook*. New York: Alfred A. Knopf, 1982.

Seddon, George. *The Mitchell Beazley Pocket Guide to Indoor Plants*. London: Mitchell Beazley Publishers, 1979.

Taylor, Norman. *Taylor's Pocket Guide to Herbs and Edible Flowers*. Rev. ed. Boston, MA: Houghton Mifflin Co., 1990.

Time Life Electronic Encyclopedia. World Wide Web. New York: Time Life, Inc., 1997.

Time Life Houseplant Pavilion. World Wide Web. New York: Time Life, Inc., 1997.

INDEX

Aphids 85

Basil 9-12
    feeding 11
    freezing 82
    harvesting and
        storing 12, 82
    history 10
    Italian 10
    lemon 10
    light requirements 11
    pinching and
        pruning 11, 63-
        64, 65
    planting 10-11
    propagating 75
    sweet 10
    symbols chart 9
    Thai 10
    watering 11

Care, basic, symbols 6
Chinese parsley 47
Chives 20-22
    feeding 22
    freezing 82
    harvesting and
        storing 22
    light requirements 21
    pinching and
        pruning 22
    planting 21
    propagating 75-76
    symbols chart 20
    watering 22
Cilantro 46-48
    Chinese parsley 47

coriander 47
    feeding 48
    freezing 82
    fresh coriander 47
    harvesting and
        storing 48, 80-81
    history 47
    light requirements 47
    pinching and
        pruning 48
    propagating 78
    symbols chart 46
    watering 48
Cleaning 64
Containers 70, 83
    dish gardens 84
    hanging 83-84
    windowsill 84
Coriander 47
    seeds 47, 48, 80-81
    fresh 47
Curly parsley 43

Decorating
    containers 83
    dish gardens 84
    hanging plants 83-84
    window sill 84
Dill 23-25
    feeding 25
    freezing 82
    harvesting and
        storing 25, 80
    history 24
    light requirements 25
    pinching and
        pruning 25

Dill, cont.
    planting 24
    propagating 78
    seeds 25, 80
    symbols chart 23
    watering 25
Drainage holes 70
Drying
    how to 80-82
    leaves 81-82
    microwave 81
    on the stem 81-82

English broad-leaf thyme
    30

Fertilizer 59-62
    amount to give 61-62
    balance 60
    basil 11
    benefits 59-60
    chives 22
    cilantro 48
    dill 25
    marjoram 41
    mint 37
    oregano 28
    parsley 44
    repotting 72
    rosemary 18
    tarragon 34
    thyme 31
    types 60-61
    young plants 78
Flat-leaf parsley 43
Freezing 82
    basil 82
    chives 82
    cilantro 82
    dill 82

ice cube trays 82
parsley 82
French narrow-leaf
    thyme 30
French summer thyme 30
French tarragon 33

Gifts 77

Harvesting and storing
    79-82
    basil 12, 82
    chives 22
    cilantro 48, 80
    coriander seed 48,
        80-81
    dill leaves 25, 80
    dill seeds 25, 80
    how to harvest 79-81
    marjoram 41
    mint 38
    oregano 28
    parsley 45
    rosemary 19
    sage 15
    tarragon 34
    thyme 31
Herb plants
    appearance 50-51
    duration symbols 7
    flavor 50-51
    how to choose 49-52
    how to succeed 1-2
    moving outside 84-85
    pests 85
    price 52
    soil condition 51
    variety 5
Herbs, uses 2-3

History
    basil 10
    cilantro 47
    dill 24
    marjoram 40
    oregano 27
    parsley 43
    rosemary 17
    sage 14
    thyme 30

Italian basil 10
Italian parsley 43

Lemon basil 10
Lemon thyme 30
Light 56-59
    benefits 57-58
    ideal 58
    rotating plant 58-59
    symbols 7
Light requirements
    basil 11
    chives 21
    cilantro 47
    dill 25
    marjoram 40
    mint 37
    oregano 28
    parsley 44
    rosemary 18
    sage 15
    tarragon 34
    thyme 31

Marjoram 39-41
    feeding 41
    harvesting and
        storing 41
    history 40

light requirements 40
pinching and
    pruning 41
planting 40
propagating 77
symbols chart 39
watering 41
Mint 35-38
    caution 37
    feeding 37
    harvesting and
        storing 38
    light requirements 37
    peppermint 36
    pinching and
        pruning 37, 63-
        65
    planting 36
    propagating 76-77
    spearmint 36
    symbols chart 35
    watering 37

Oregano 26-28
    feeding 28
    harvesting and
        storing 28
    history 27
    light requirements 28
    pinching and
        pruning 28, 63-
        64
    planting 27
    propagating 76
    symbols chart 26
    watering 28

Parsley 42-45
    Chinese 47
    curly 43

Parsley, cont.
    feeding 44
    flat-leaf 43
    freezing 82
    harvesting and
        storing 45
    history 43
    Italian 43
    light requirements 44
    pinching and
        pruning 44
    propagating 78
    symbols chart 42
    watering 44
Peppermint 36
Pests 85
    aphids 85
    spider mites 85
    whiteflies 85
Photosynthesis 57
Pinching, how to 63-65
Pinching and pruning 62-
    66
    basil 11, 63-64, 65
    benefits 62-63
    chives 22
    cilantro 48
    dill 25
    marjoram 41
    mint 37, 63-65
    oregano 28, 63-64,
        66
    parsley 44
    rosemary 18, 65-66
    sage 15
    tarragon 34
    thyme 31, 65-66
Propagating 73-78
    basil 75
    benefits 73

chives 75-76
cilantro 78
dill 78
gifts 77
marjoram 77
mint 76-77
oregano 76
parsley 78
root division 73, 74-
    75
rosemary 75
sage 75
stem cuttings 73-74
tarragon 76
thyme 76
time required 78
Prostrate rosemary 17

Repotting 69-72
    benefits 70
    fertilizer 72
    how to 70-72
    watering 71-72
    when to 70
Root division 73, 74-75
Rooting hormone
    powder 74
Rosemarinus 17
Rosemary 16-19
    feeding 18
    harvesting and
        storing 19
    history 17
    light requirements 18
    pinching and
        pruning 18, 65-
        66
    planting 17-18
    propagating 75
    prostrate 17

Rosemary, cont.
    rosemarinus 17
    symbols chart 16
    watering 18

Sage 13-15
    harvesting and
        storing 15
    history 14
    light requirements 15
    pinching and
        pruning 15
    planting 14
    propagating 75
    symbols chart 13
    watering 15
Seed planting 67-69
    basil 10
    dill 24
    marjoram 40
    oregano 27
    parsley 44
    seedlings 68, 69
Soil
    condition 51
    potting, commercial
        70-71
Spearmint 36
Spider mites 85
Starter plants 52
    basil 10
    chives 21
    cilantro 47
    dill 24
    mint 36
    oregano 27
    parsley 44
    rosemary 17-18
    sage 14
    tarragon 33

thyme 30
Stem cuttings 73-74
Storing
    dried leaves 82
    seeds 81
Sweet basil 10
Symbols
    basic care 6
    light 7
    plant duration 7
    water 6

Tarragon 32-34
    feeding 34
    French 33
    harvesting and
        storing 34
    light requirements 34
    pinching and
        pruning 34
    planting 33
    propagating 76
    symbols chart 32
    watering 34
    winter 33
Temperature extremes,
    damage 59
Thai basil 10
Thyme 29-31
    common 30
    English broad-leaf 30
    feeding 31
    French narrow-leaf
        30
    French summer 30
    harvesting and
        storing 31
    history 30
    lemon 30
    light requirements 31

Thyme, cont.
    pinching and
        pruning 31, 65-
        66
    planting 30
    propagating 76
    symbols chart 29
    watering 31

Water 53-56
    benefits 53
    extremes,
        symptoms 57
    flavor 55
    how to 54-55
    kind 55
    overwatering 53-54
    symbols 6
    when to 56
Watering
    basil 11
    chives 22
    cilantro 48
    dill 25
    marjoram 41
    mint 37
    oregano 28
    parsley 44
    rosemary 18
    sage 15
    tarragon 34
    thyme 31
Whiteflies 85
Winter tarragon 33